E F G H I J

N O P Q

W X Y Z

ABC
Book
of
Feelings

To Jess, Amy, and Nathan

Copyright © 1991 Concordia Publishing House
3558 S. Jefferson Avenue, St. Louis, MO 63118-3968
Manufactured in the United States of America

Library of Congress Cataloging - in - Publication Data

Boddy, Marlys.
    ABC book of feelings / by Marlys Boddy ; illustrated by Joe Boddy.

    Summary: Uses a Christian perspective to explore the world of emotions alphabetically, from afraid to zany.
    ISBN 0-570-04190-2
    1. Emotions -- Juvenile literature. 2. Emotions -- Religious aspects -- Christianity -- Juvenile literature. 3. English language -- Alphabet -- Juvenile literature. [1. Emotions. 2. Christian life. 3. Alphabet.] I. Boddy, Joe, ill. II. Title.
BF561.B63 1991
152.4 -- dc20   90-46340
[E]   CIP
                                       AC

3 4 5 6 7 8 9 10 11 12   03 02 01 00 99 98 97 96 95 94

ABC
BOOK OF FEELINGS

by Marlys Boddy
illustrated by Joe Boddy

God gave everyone feelings,
And they're important too!
No matter how old you are,
They're still a part of you.
Can you share your feelings?
Why don't you try and see?
Here are some good ideas,
Starting from A to Z.

Afraid . . . Afraid is how you feel when you think something might hurt you.

Bashful...

Bashful is how you feel when everyone is looking at you, and you wish they wouldn't.

Curious ...
**Curious is how you feel
when you want to find
out about things.**

Disappointed…
Disappointed is how
you feel when things
don't happen the way
you want them to.

Encouraged ...

Encouraged is how you feel when you keep going because you know that God and others will help you make it.

F

Foolish...
**Foolish is how you feel
when you've done something
that was kind of silly.**

Grateful ...
**Grateful is how you feel
when someone has done
something nice for you.**

Homesick ...
Homesick is how you feel when you're away from home, and you miss your family and friends.

Impatient ...

Impatient is how you feel when you have to wait, and you don't want to.

Jealous ...
Jealous is how you feel
when you wish you had
something that belongs
to someone else.

Kind ...
**Kind is how you feel
when you are caring
and helpful to others.**

Lonesome …
Lonesome is how you feel when you're all alone but wish you weren't.

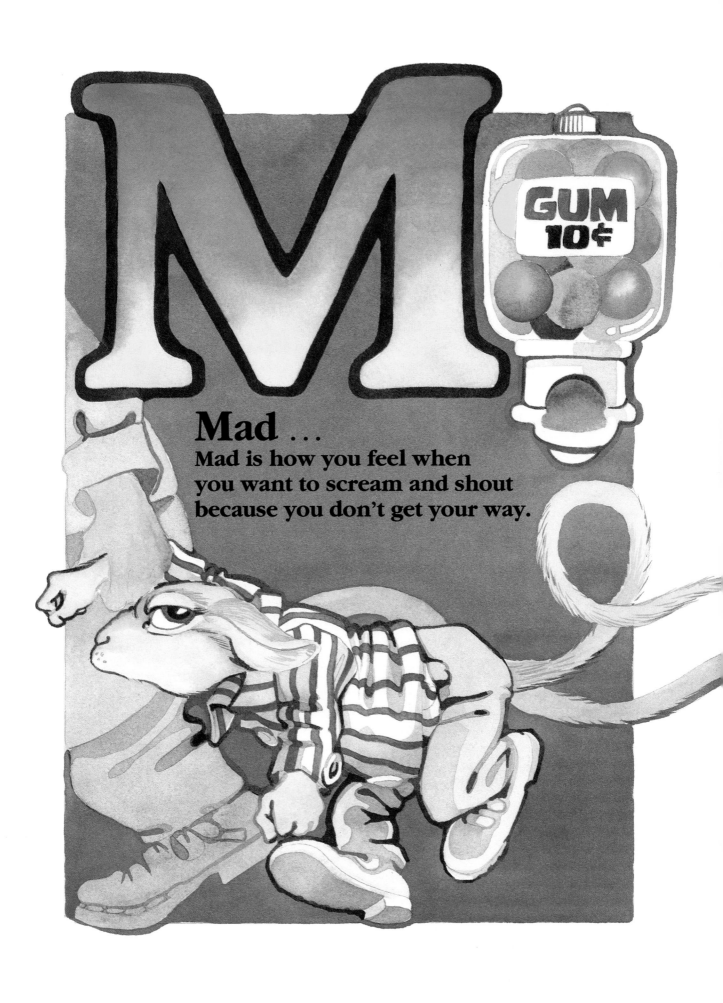

Mad …

Mad is how you feel when
you want to scream and shout
because you don't get your way.

GUM
10¢

Neglected . . .
Neglected is how you
feel when no one pays
any attention to you.

Offended ...
Offended is how you
feel when someone
has hurt your feelings.

Puzzled . . .
Puzzled is how you
feel when you don't
know the answer
to a problem.

Quarrelsome...
Quarrelsome is how you feel
when you want to start
a fight with someone.

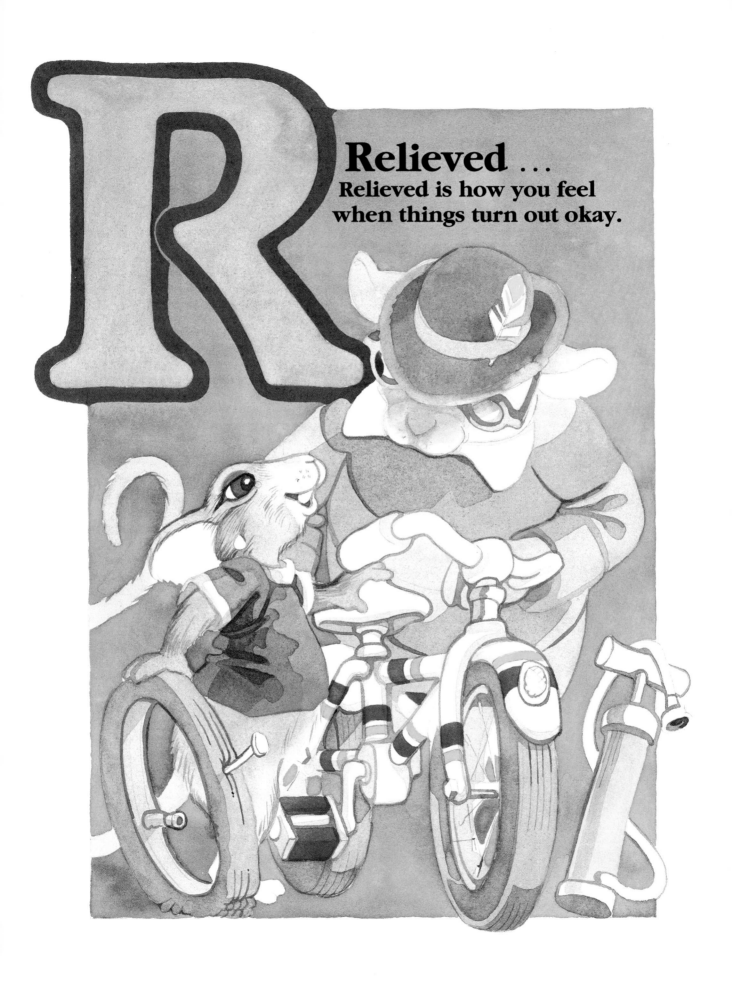

Relieved ...
Relieved is how you feel
when things turn out okay.

Surprised...
Surprised is how you feel when something happens that you didn't expect.

Trusting ...

Trusting is how you feel when you know you can depend on God and others.

Useful . . .
Useful is how you
feel when you think
that somebody needs you.

V

Venturesome...
Venturesome is how you
feel when you do something
new and daring.

Worried...
Worried is how you feel when you're not sure that everything will be all right.

eXcited…
Excited is how you feel
when something great
is going to happen.

Yucky...
Yucky is how you feel
when nothing seems
to be any good.

Zany... Zany is how you
feel when you act silly to make
other people laugh.

It's okay to have feelings.
They're God's gift, you know.
They help you understand yourself
No matter where you go.
God cares about your feelings,
What you think and do.
He helps you care for others;
They have feelings too!

Dear Parent:

Feelings are an important part of our human relationships. By understanding our feelings, we learn more about ourselves. By sharing our feelings, we help others to learn more about us. We hope the ABC Book of Feelings will help your children express some "feeling" words.

As you read this book, allow your children to choose a page to talk about. Ask them how they think the little mice feel. Have they ever felt the same way? Listen to their feelings with patience and understanding.

Remind your children that God loves them. He gave them feelings to enrich their lives, and He is always willing to forgive them when their feelings cause them to hurt others. Explain that Jesus understands our feelings, because as true man, He felt them too! By accepting our children with all their feelings and emotions, we show them the kind of love God has for all of us.

Sincerely,

Marlys and Joe Boddy